GW00492683

Introduction

BONUS

60 FREE Mandala designs to print. Go to the last page to see the link to the PDF. The book has a good mix of beautiful Mandalas. Enough patterns for a long time of coloring fun!

Relaxing & Meditation

Mandalas are originally from Buddhism. They have a meditative and relaxing effect on the viewer. That is why mandala designs are so popular. When painting, you can completely relax and recharge your batteries. Forget the worries of the stressful everyday life and let yourself be completely on the respective pattern.

Lost Time

Get free from time pressure and commitments. Do not set a time limit for the coloring book pages and resist the urge to finish quickly.

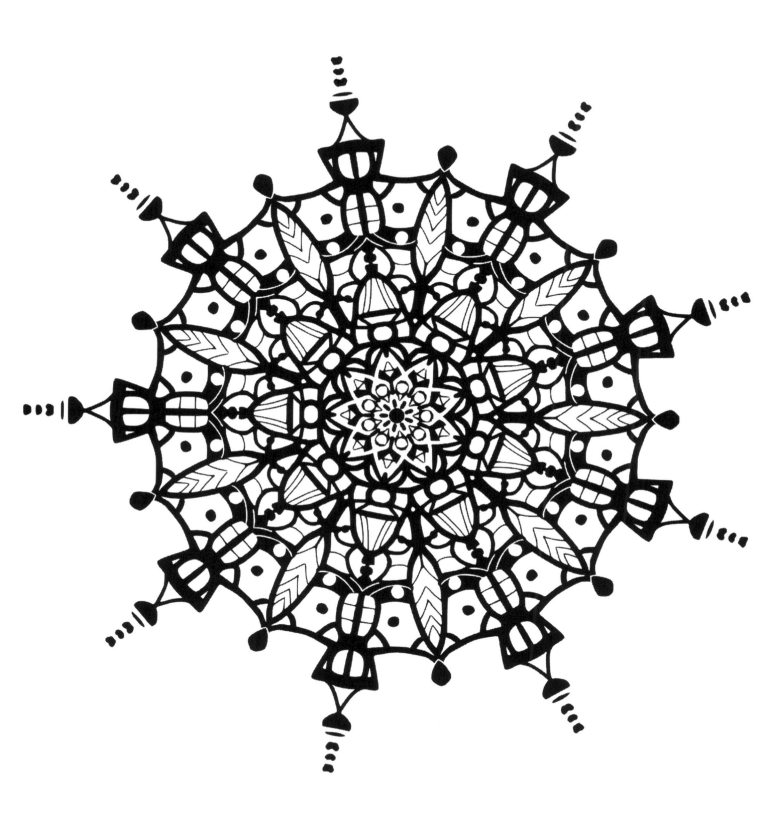

Review our Book...

 If you like our Mandala colouring book it would be very nice if you leave us a review on Amazon!

 ## YOUR BONUS

60 FREE Mandala designs to print. The book has a good mix of beautiful Mandalas. Enough patterns for a long time of coloring fun! Go to https://goo.gl/4z4e0C to download/print the PDF.

© 2017 Malbuch-fuer-Erwachsene.org
All rights reserved
CreateSpace Independent Publishing Platform

Alexander Topolewski
Hauswörmannsweg 25
49082 Osnabrück

ISBN-13: 978-1544799414
ISBN-10: 1544799411

21441501R00048

Printed in Great Britain
by Amazon